What Will Keep Us Alive

Sundress Publications • Knoxville, TN

ISBN: 978-1-939675-25-5

Published by Sundress Publications

Editor: Erin Elizabeth Smith

erin@sundresspublications.com

http://www.sundresspublications.com

Colophon: This book is set in Kaiti TC.

Cover Design: Mary Ellen Knight

Cover Image: "Night Watch" by Maggie Taylor (www.maggietaylor.com)

Book Design: Erin Elizabeth Smith

Special Thanks: Jane Huffman, T.A. Noonan, & Hunter Parsons

What Will Keep Us Alive

Kristin LaTour

Acknowledgements

The following poems were published in earlier versions in the following:

Adanna: "Life Still," "The Dowager's Poem"

Adroit Journal: "Her Husband's Fishing"

Atticus Review: "When Billy Collins Falls for Me"

Cider Press Review: "To My Friend Who Pets Bees in Her Garden," "Lot's Young Wife"

Connotation Press: "Fortune"

Dirtcakes: "How Myths Begin"

Escape into Life: "Barnacles"

Fifth Wednesday Journal: "The Human Cannonball Recalls His Boyhood"

Menacing Hedge: "Sibling," "Stars Made of Salt," "She Stops to Sew"

The Museum of Americana: "Rows," "Caring for a Hoosier," "Farming Depression"

Popshot: "Malady"

qarrtsiluni: "Agoraphobia"

Rufous City Review: "This Long Winter"

San Pedro Review: "Why the Garcias Never Attended the Circus after 1942"

Stirring: A Literary Collection: "Counting Her Sorrows," "Little Witch"

TAB: "Thimblerigger"

Selections from the collection also appeared in the chapbooks *Agoraphobia* from dancing girl press and *Blood* from Naked Mannekin Press.

Table of Contents

Part Three

To Paul, who has cast a spell on me

even though he professes to not be a witch.

Part One

Agoraphobia

There can be no fear where notes
ring true. The cello's clear G after A
will overshadow your tears, the audience
will swell in the current of the melody.
Sway with your eyes shut tight
and everything will disappear. Call
the music to you like the beekeeper
spins honey— golden, sticky, sweet.

Change the music, little girl;
call the notes from the diaphragm
inside a honeycomb nest.
Find some beautiful shades of Naples yellow.
See? Even the electric bees
tingle with symphonies.

Savanna Lullaby

Here is the soft click of the clock's arms
as it winds through the darkening hours,
and here is the lion with soft fur that guarded you
as you played in the jungle of your yard.
Listen to the clock like the heartbeat of your lion;
your own lion's heart will be brave in darkness.

Breathe in the savanna night
blown in through the window, mixed with the breath
of the impalas, zebras who sleep and wait for you.
Your dreams will be of shallow watering holes.
The sun moves so slowly, time almost begins.

Eve Chooses Her Fruit

The aproned Serpent stands by
arranging his little tree-covered stand
as Eve chooses her fruit.

She tests the first's firmness with a thumb.
The skin gives and juice dribbles
down her wrist. She licks the tracks.

The next is the highest in reach.
She examines the skin
for spots, presses it to her nose.
But there's no scent—
she tosses it away like a ball.

The last is tucked under the canopy,
close to the thick branches.
Firm enough, smelling sweet,
rosy as cheeks, she takes it
in her small, dirty hands,
presses it smooth
to her parted lips
testing the give against teeth.

The Serpent nods his approval
as her eyes roll back, her tongue
licks the juice from her lips.

Barbie Fucked Up My Life

Not because of her curves and concavities
beyond any capacity evolution ever cooked up
for wasps and ants. Or the way she can drive
young girls to stand naked in front of full-length mirrors,
suck in their guts, stick out their chests.

Not because of little boys' curiosity
of what's inside her, peeking under
her head, in the cavity hidden at her hip.
I never understood why my friends screamed
after finding their dolls dismembered.

Not from the violence of dressing her,
forcing tights onto her splayed legs,
yanking a comb through her sinfully long hair.

It was that she was forbidden
the way Erica Jong's novels were—
hidden away in my mother's nightstand
with their orgasms and areolas,
always just out of reach
like candy at the corner store,
the answers to word problems.
My mother's gentle *No* every time
I wrote Barbie's name in perfect cursive
on Christmas wish lists.

Practical Plastic Surgery

Cutting isn't difficult.

It's the knack of a scalpel.

Practice on an orange with an X-ACTO knife,

through the skin,

                don't nick the pulp.

When you have perfected this,

try slicing tendons, sewing them back together.

A chicken wing will do, the small

bands holding it in that neat triangle.

Next, saw bone with a serrated knife,

maybe an oxtail or pork chop.

Reset it,

                pull the muscle back in place,

then cast it in plastic wrap.

You're ready to use a woman now.

Just decide what needs to be fixed.

You know how deep to cut,

but you'll have to staunch her bleeding on the fly.

It's easy; just mop it up.

Trim tendons so her limbs curl like wings.

You may need to shorten bones for grace's sake,

but secure in your skills, saw away.

Gently pat her flesh back, sew stitches so straight,

make sure the tape on her skin is clean and neat.

Don't worry that we skipped anesthesia,

over scarring and internal bleeding.

We'll cover that next time.

For now, pray.

Prayer heals all things.

Sibling

You call me to say your pencil drawing was well received, but the watercolor didn't come out right. You sniffle and pause; I know this is not the reason you called me—

You say you can't remember whole passages of your childhood. They seem redacted, like charcoal smeared over the thick pages of your past.

I tell you about the time we made small piles of leaves under the cottonwood trees, beds for our dolls. A whole nursery of blankets, a pot to heat bottles. We nurtured our babies for an autumn afternoon as the sun's light filtered through the sparse branches.

Guns, Blood and Water

The puppy had to learn
What is taken away will be returned
the bone in his mouth
retrieved by Mother's hand,

but having mistaken thumb for bone
his tooth cut through like butter
blood on the bone
on his tongue.

And Sister running for bandages
and Mother at the sink running water—
blood and water mixing

Father getting the gun
Brother at the door
Sister down the hall
Mother at the sink
Dog with his bone

Gun at the dog's skull
as he chewed the marrow
licked the blood—
safety off
Brother's *No*

blood and water

bullet in the chamber

No

gun cocked and ready

at *No*, gun lifting

from dog's skull

to Brother's heart

Mother at the sink

Sister there with bandages

Father with the gun

Brother with the *No*

Gun, blood, water, *No*

Why the Garcias Never Attended the Circus after 1942

Great Aunt Esperanza

tired of the south Texas sun

and her job at her father's dusty grocery:

the feel of tomatoes she piled in pyramids

and the dumb numbers on the register.

All the boring Catholic boys

wanted to fix engines and make babies

not the ruckus that ran in her veins.

She snuck away with a carney one May,

came back ten autumns later with

tattoos of cherry petals on her cheeks

stories of trapeze artists

who swung her glittering heart.

She scrubbed elephant hides with long brushes

before the parades through small Midwestern towns.

Her hair spangled with the confetti

of water from the clowns' water pails.

Brushing cobwebs off her old bed frame,

She stuffed her mattress with sawdust and popcorn,

tried to have dreams of girls in pink

on milk white horses,

drank only icy lemonade.

Spidergirl

Spidergirl's power was no accident. She stuck her hand
in the webby cage and grasped her destiny,

watched the bubbling bite.

Spidergirl doesn't spin webs. She crochets them
like sticky doilies trapping criminals with her craft.

Her whiplash wit stings.

Spidergirl doesn't get a pixie cut, doesn't fasten down
her breasts to avoid tight situations. Her identity is still

safe behind the mask, curls or no.

Spidergirl knows the intricate tangent between skyscrapers
and the parabola curve of her flight from one to the other.

She has no trouble in the dark.

Spidergirl can take a sock and a pow, bounce back after
being thrown into a wall or through a window.

She knows she was born in blood.

Fortune

Look for fortune where it is least expected, at the crossroad of

pain and opportunity.

~ Chinese Fortune

Girl couldn't stand the click of Father's false teeth

against his gums, the smell of smoke

that clung to his clothes and yellow tongue,

the way the sweet stench could adhere

to her hair, how she'd have to peel off

its stickiness like sap in the bath.

Father said Girl's face was severe, her

sloped nose and slash of a mouth, when his cheek

was close to her own. The door cracked open

and light spread like broken yolks.

Mother was always sloppy, dropping plates,

making grotesque patterns of gravy over

dishes' decal flowers—greasy brown and petal pink—

Girl's stomach tightened every supper. Not even

Little Sister, with her plump plum cheeks,

straight-toothed smile was safe. Father's palm

pressed down her chestnut curls while her eyes

cracked like porcelain teacups. Had Girl been able

to read her horoscope in Father's paper,

she would have choked on laughter.

The Summer Her Boyfriend Suffered Lycanthropy

This is what comes from growing up
in a ghost town. They sit outside out to watch

lights swirl the desert night.
She wants to feel his hand on the small

of her back, his claws beastly in the best way.
She chews her cheek and waits for the sky to be erased.

What they become when they are alone are branches
like a river parting in channels.

The breeze is a breath on her neck,
is a language she can't understand.

If the stars were counting beads, they'd know
how long they've been here, how long there is

to stay. When he suggests leaving, her tongue gets cut
on her teeth. She wants a release like thunder.

When their parents abandoned them for the trains
that came from the east, they understood what love

meant. The creek kept flowing, so they had water to drink.
They could have tried Houston, or San Antonio

but like wooden cabins, independence was new

and ready to stand a while longer. The graves were still

marked by wooden crosses when they waved the last wagon

goodbye. How little it took to wash their town away.

She was born under the sign of Cancer. They can't recall

his exact age, the color his hair was at birth. She asks

him to howl. The thunder rumbles. They never asked

to be born into this nothingness, the smell of dust.

On The Days She Becomes a Bee

The Victrola sings out of its horn
soprano piano and brass
filling the room like a jelly roll
with sweetness and sway.

She spends the morning concocting
in the yellow kitchen. Bubbling jams
and seed-dappled glazes steam
above blue flames in copper saucepans.

She bumbles down hallways, walls
combed with frames, oil paintings
of fat infants and sleek saplings
supposed to infuse her with youth.

The mice skedaddle and stagger
drunken on dairy to the bedroom's
four poster bed to giggle and twitter
as her feet slip past the bedskirt.

It's not as if she's never curbed a taste
for sweets, turned knobs on doors salty
with memories. The stones she throws
into glassy ponds ripple, remind her

of tables covered in glassware

her grandmother's white whipped potatoes

bowls of globby turnips

dry pork loins left cold on platters.

She licks her fingers, sticky with honey,

and crushes the walnuts for baklava.

The window frames a meadow of milkweed.

butterflies. Tonight it will flicker firefly.

Moving West

She packed her cauldron,
the dried woodland flowers,
the cat's tail in a secret suitcase.
The car headed west from
land that smelled of iron ore,
septic rivers. She nodded, napped,
dreamed of lithe blue birds as tall as ostriches
sand in dunes, in crevices, laying flat against
horizons of red rock.

Each stop was more plateau-like:
Illinois' barely-hills of coal,
Missouri's glacial mounds,
Oklahoma's wasteland.
They slept under the canopy
of a Chevette, rocked by wind,
rain or still as a casket.
She murmured spells when he entered her
under trees, the roots
taking his seed into their veins
blessing their spring branches
with abundant blossoms.

When they arrived in the summer Sonoran heat
she found the suitcase was empty

but her lover swore on her breast
he knew nothing, less than that.
She went to the barrio, but found only
clay pots for sale, decorative and gaudy,
just Mexican oregano, sage, yucca flowers.

She couldn't abide lying under creosote
or palo verde, so she and her lover took
to clean muslin sheets on a spring bed
that sang songs like sea-shanties
as they came together. Her murmurs
slurred, made her incantations meaningless
garble under an adobe roof. It wasn't long
before her womb closed.

The Mid-western spells she memorized
slipped into unlabeled envelopes. Her hands
forgot how to move over a steaming pot,
were blistered more than once. She
seasoned everything with chiles.
The baby was born while she lay on her back
without friends to support a standing birth.
It cried in colic and frustration at the spice
in its mother's milk. She wanted to cover it
in tattoos of what remaining spells she recalled.
Cactus needles were useless and her ink
wouldn't stay black.

Retablo at the Altar of Santa Frida

Derecha

Dry, unwashed, porcelain cold.

Leather stiff from sweat, unbloodied.

The belief that men could rule themselves.

Sticks meant for walking, not herding.

Unseen, the blue water and toes

a volcano choking on love, stopped

with progress. A whole woman, a dress,

floating separate, pale skin, red silk.

Above, a green parrot, perching

on embroidered Campeche flowers.

Siniestra

Sinister plaster, chest-shaped, thick.

False limbs, shoed in tooled red leather.

Traps and cages for a woman's spine

broken, twisted. The straps loosened.

The straps fastened. The breath escaped.

The faceless unborn. The sickle and hammer

red and unswung. Metal hinged. Behind

the hint of a monkey's fur, a golden rebozo.

Centro

Lace fit to adorn angels, sewn to skirts.

A huipil embroidered with black-edged flowers.

Every thread and stitch a synapse, a brush

stroke. Camisoles in cotton as fine as gauze.

Earrings of silver teardrops, turquoise birds.

Coral beaded necklaces, pearls, carved shells.

The more pain, the more beautiful her dresses.

The more suffering, the more ribbons in her hair.

Her Knack for Flicking Matches

You buy so much kerosene I smell it
in your hair spread like anemone over
the cotton sheets. In the evening light

I love watching you sip Molotov cocktails
and cook vindaloo, the fat in the pan sputtering.
Our kisses almost kill me, electric chair thrill.

Your best dress is covered in blood, shimmering
red and slick against your lean leg. I'm almost
afraid. I'm almost to the point of kissing my crucifix.

Your laugh is like the end of a cigarette, raw
deep. I'm almost always being careful,
my steps quiet and a little shaky. I wonder why

you never remove your ruby earrings, why
you look directly at the sun, why
no one meets your gaze.

I'm almost ready to save my own
pieces of pie. I'm almost ready to add
emergency contacts who are strangers.

Your words are spread before you like piano keys.
Pianos are made of wood.
I used to think my heart was too.

I'm almost about to make one last swipe across the counter.

I'm about to take one last breath. I'm about to.

I pocket your matches. I'm the bridge.

Lot's Young Wife

1.

When he met her, she was called Edith, happiness,
but whatever joy had been at her naming
was long gone. He sometimes called her Diynah
when she would judge his handiwork and click her teeth,
or Miryam for her stubbornness when she wanted
to buy the best lamp oil, perfume for her hair.
At her worst, when she chose to stay away hours
in baths or listening to musicians in the dirty street,
he called her Bara or Acantha, while wringing his hands.
That night she was Adrasteia, not wanting to run away.

2.

When he trudged back, he knew she wasn't any of these.
He lifted her with a grunt and the hem of her robe cracked,
so he called her Adiiuu as a joke,
since she was no longer light,
and Eidel as he pushed her towards his new home,
delicate and breakable, too fragile for raindrops.
His daughters were amazed and frightened. The brave one,
who missed her mother's laughter,
called her Libnah as she caressed
the white wrists. Another stayed by the hearth and muttered
Zakiya, knowing her purity was false.

Lot, on a good day, called her Yerusha, his possession,

as he broke off fingertips for the soup or filed away pinches

of her hair for dough. Most days, he called her what she was.

How to Survive in the Sonoran Desert

dust can be gathered from the wind

rubbed generously into the soles

fur from tarantulas will bring on nightfall

every red barrel cactus flower

reads like a sundial or a compass

a dizzy ant is a sign of impending shade

water is where you look for it

never where it seems to be

God can make granite weep

How Myths Begin

Children sucked in stomachs to count ribs,

nipples like flattened berries,

and they paused to ask aloud, why,

and why again.

Their mother looked to the sky,

counted the clouds,

picked up a stone,

began another story.

Part Two

Recipe for a Star

Mix samson blue and madison pink
in a glass jar with a zinc lid. Whisper

through a Turkish grille carved with six-pointed
hexagrams and topped with onion domes. Each layer

of an onion is a universe. Your body
holds the dust of an ancient particle that flew

across space, somehow landed
in your mother's womb.

Your whisper must include words
like polyphony and panoply, zenith and azimuth.

Set the jar behind a barn that was once
painted red, whose door hangs ajar

like a boy's almost-pulled tooth.
Walk to the east, past the oaks to the cottonwoods

that lean over the river like broken men.
Gather the flecks of sunlight that ripple

over the lazy water into the pocket of an apron.
Let the sparkle fall from your fingers;

wait like a galaxy, a small universe unbounded.

Little Witch

She can control the wind if she stands on the porch

or cement steps leading to a house's back door,

holding her arms aloft, squinting her eyes.

Mostly she likes the air to be still, barely rustling.

Empty notebooks have demons, so she chooses

spiral bound, blue covers, pages filled

with scribbles in red crayon and the hard-pressed

handwriting of girls learning penmanship.

These are the spells that send small poltergeists

scrambling. She curses her siblings with their dirt-

filled ears, saliva-crusted mouths. She blesses her father

who leaves more often than he returns and scolds

her mother when her belly swells again. She can see

her future, her hair turning to Twizzlers everyone will want

to pull from her head and her words precious as trinkets

hidden in a box: broken bits of jewelry, a beetle's leg, one tiny

doll's shoe, a blue marble. People will want to look

into her mouth. She already plans to hide in a corn crib

and live like a cat. Listen. She's practicing her purr.

Palisades

Never walk carelessly on rocky
ledges like these. One bad step
and you'll feel the wind in a new way,
reeling past blue sky to what you thought. . .

No—

you were wrong. Not water, but rocks
orange in the blue and white waves.
Returning, the cliff

                    will no longer

                              tether you;

                   your blood

howls in your ears.

Wonderful how the last moment breezes
east to Sault Ste. Marie.

                You remember there's no
salt here,

       the sting of hitting will be only broken bone.

Through it all, stay in the car,
admire the pines bending south
rounded clouds racing over them and you.
There is no danger here, the engine
shut off. Only breath, static, and the freezing cold.

Family Tree

The roots gnarl and lurch. See the open
mouths chewing chicken, the empty bourbon bottles
abandoned at the trunk, an uncle staggering
into the house after a white cotton dress.

That stunted branch cut off for sanity's sake;
he removed his cousins' hands and placed them
palms up on ice in the picnic basket. Left to bleed,
they missed their mamas, the biscuits and honey.

See the swing missing a rope, made from broken boards
stolen from the neighbor's barn. Recall the night the fathers
knotted a noose, dragged the girl screaming from her bed,
so she could watch her lover burning.

Topmost twigs bifurcate and twist
and a boy fights off the small hands reaching
from the window. His sister, a doll with hollow eyes,
can only wait, hum, stare at her shoes.

Into the World Came a Soul Named Ida

after Ivan Albright's painting cir. 1930

No one taught her at Sunday school
that Jesus loves her more than anything,
that sin can be redeemed and forgiven.
Or that her name in Latin means
diligent and hardworking.
She'd laugh without irony in her steel cut
voice if she knew. Had her Irish mother
explained in Gaelic Ida means thirsty,
she might have gone hoarse with laughter.

She once had fresh cash to spend
and a cut crystal and silver dresser set
but now is left with a cracked mirror.
Her skin is pock-marked, bulging
pale and rouged with lipstick.
Her blonde bob is badly cut,
her pencil skirt ill-fitting.

Men no longer bring her blooms.
Her veins blossom on thick-stemmed legs.
Her vases gather only weeds
she drunkenly picks.

Her life is pencil-scribbled lists
of things she'll never buy.

Her cigarette has almost burned out

like the matches that litter the floor.

Even if Jesus would forgive her,

she's forgotten how to bend her knees that way.

She never knew how to ask.

Time to Start Over

We moved west in search of open spaces where our spells wouldn't catch in branches or stick in webs. A good spell and its smoke should reach the sky. We gathered our books, seeds, a squirrel, several cats and bartered a wagon with jam.

This wood is of the earth
The earth touches our feet
Our hands stir the air
Let us breathe in sky

Indiana had good streams and clay. We dug our hut facing south, hung the cauldron over the fire, set the squirrel loose and stroked the cats. The first full moon we blessed the land sky and water, made fire from flint, danced naked and blossoming under withering clouds. It was a good omen.

Our feet mix with earth
Our breasts round like the moon
The flame blesses our prayers
The flame lifts our song

This is where we can be free, in open space with cattle, a large framed house. We don't kill every man who comes, nor do we set evil on other women. Our hums as we sleep soothe towns whole miles away.

We give praise for peace and plenty.

We cast spells for light-shining joy.

We are of the earth, water, sky.

We sing branches and beaches, our memory.

Caring for a Hoosier

Remember it was once rooming house
for spices and flour, dishes, pie pans, string.
Think of it like Chicago or Milwaukee's
immigrant neighborhoods
where everyone spoke their native tongue.
The flour nestled in with baking powder and soda.
The measuring spoons and cups shared a drawer.
One shelf was all spices, whispering their secrets through
zinc tops. Like all cities, things break.
The handle for the sugar bin was lost.
The rear leg gave in to termites or water damage.
Everyone moved away, and now the cups live
in cupboards, the brown sugar in a vacuum-sealed canister in
a place called the pantry.

There is always room for renewal.
Take the Hoosier home to the backyard and strip it, stain it,
mend its legs and drawers. Wait years searching for the right
handle, the missing jars. Meet a blacksmith who can fix the sifter.
Buy a crumbling cookbook, look up recipes for biscuits.
Set jars of homemade jam on the shelf.
Listen for the languages that were just waiting,
never silent, never gone.

Marriage Advice

Marrying into a coven isn't advised
since your mother in-law might ask you
to flay a baby, dip its legs in flour then egg
then flour again. Season with salt then pepper
Fry until crisp. She will hum
if you ask whose it is, where it came from.

Your father in-law may call you
to the rafters with him, legs dangling,
to sing wordless songs in the dust, chew
the old wood, shove splinters in your shoes—
protection against pitchforks, pistols, fire.

You may find your husband's
sisters have stolen one or maybe two
of your teeth while you slept with your mouth
agape, your arm around your husband's waist
so they leaned over him, rested their arms
on his chest, naked and warm, breathing.

You will bring home a pet, before you have a baby,
but each will go missing after you've left
for something simple like milk, the paper.
Come back to find the front door open
even though you locked it, latched it
whispering the words your husband told you

would keep you safe, but he's nowhere now.

Even relatives come back from
the dead, some afterlife they never visit
from under the dirt of the basement
their bones creaking and cracking,
teeth loose and looking like yours,
their breath always cold. They want
to hug you, hold you, know if you are carrying
their future in your hidden places.

No matter what spells he cast on you about love
about how the tingling in your chest is magic
or the touch of your fingers laced in his
is an unending bond, you need to find your own
old leather book, translate the pages of runes
into something that saves you.
Take your golden eggs, escape the garden.
Release all the dogs and run.

The Thimblerigger

She knows all about pricks and punctures
the danger of points and pins, needles
and cacti. Have you ever tried to dust
the skin of a succulent spiked with spines?
She understands, carries the tiniest bandages
and all manner of fingertip protection.
Leather snoods to snug over index fingers,
metal caps dotted with perforations perfect
for pushing needles through canvas.
Her pockets overflow with several sizes:
tiny like a baby's curled pinky, to the largest man's thumb.
So many ways a hand can be hurt. Crushed in
train couplings, smashed in carriage doors,
pinched in door jambs, gashed in metal gears.
She knows her work will never be done,
her own fingers missing their distal phlanxes,
her wings serving double function, delivering
her thimbles and carrying her from house to house.

Life Still

after Preston Dickinson's "Still Life in Interior," 1920

This is her life still:

her blue table,

tea and sake.

Her love of lemons and clocks,

the magazines she won't read,

dwarfed by chairs whose laps

she never curls into.

Her vases are artfully placed

on shelf and mantle

but never hold flowers.

She lets the dust settle

turning all but the lemons gray.

Rows

every cement marker two feet
high and five inches square
shows where once each spring
sowers planted seeds an arching
turn each row promised survival
four maybe five generations like
rows of corn alfalfa soybeans
acre upon acre seas green
and leaves sprinkled with yellow
flowers and years rain sun
sometimes floods sometimes drought worry
and then reaping another winter
snow covered fields row markers
like headstones buried hope again

Farming Depression

Ticking is torn and stained.

Violets won't even bloom.

Cream in coffee curdles

fermenting like bad dreams.

You comb my tangled hair

after I nick your neck

shaving swaths with a straight edge.

Cubic feet is how we

measure this frame house life,

reaping dust and apples.

"Get off my land" painted

in your sloppy whitewash.

Ask me. Ask me again.

Break me like a stained cup.

Advent, Milkweed

In winter, the pods are spilt open,
wombs halved and empty;
the seeds gone on fall wind
and buried in currents of snow—
what was full to bursting and then
suddenly nothing but air.

There is nothing in unfilling,
finding room again for something new
or changing from seed nest to rodent's home,
from Christmas to Epiphany.

Barren is the mind that labeled Sarah
Rebekah, and Rachel.
Barren was Mary
as her son bled on his cross.

A womb that was fluid-full
or blood-ready, now stills
for another month of filling.
To call it barren is like calling
a cloudless sky barren.
The cast iron kettle barren
because it is poured out.

Counting Her Sorrows

She rowed her dozen sorrows
to the center of the lake
pushed them each overboard
hoping they'd drown,
but they floated, grew
arms or fins and swam
in the wake back to shore,
shook the wet from their skin.
They clambered into her car,
blank stares and *ahems*
the whole way home.

She walked her 24 sorrows
to the ocean-battered cliff
tossed them off one by one,
but they boomeranged back
faster than her arm
could throw and counting them
as they huddled at her feet
she sighed, led the slow parade
back over the hill to her darkened home.

She packaged her 36 sorrows
in brown cardboard boxes
wrapped in brown paper

tied with white twine.

She licked 36 stamps and

addressed the labels

to prisoners at the island penitentiary.

The boxes were traced

back to her door

where they were delivered,

smashed and full

of hungry squinting sorrows, only more.

She boarded her 48 sorrows

on the train that crossed

mountains, savannas,

valleys covered in snow

arranged them in reclining seats

with cups of tea

and one shortbread cookie each.

She took a long rope

laced it between them as

they munched and slurped

took the other end with her

off the train just before

the conductor shut it tight.

She tied the rope

around her slender waist,

held her breath, closed her eyes.

Part Three

She Stops to Sew

She brushes sand from wet skin,
finds an edge along her forearm,
peels clockwise from the thumb side
to the back and folds it into a neat square,
sets down her coffee cup,
leaves a circle stain around a black tattooed bird.
It smells like cinnamon and chocolate,
reminds her of Paris café afternoons
and street-side flower sellers.

From her sole, the second length
is cloud-transparent,
grey and a little green like feathers falling
downy to the floor before pinning its edge
to the first swath, steel conjoining flesh.
She sketches a room on the top of her foot
small sweeps of ink,
a piano and a window.

A length from her cheek is like parchment,
muslin, music— Appalachian
full of timbre and twang.
She smudges coal dust on her thigh,
hums a melody flat as a mountain top.

She stops to sip water and make a list

of bodices: sweetheart, empire, corset, boat.

She threads a note-shaped needle before beginning

at her throat and peeling down to her belly,

finding her grandmother's flocked pink wallpaper:

seahorses chasing algae swirls.

This is where she stops,

at the edge of a beach,

to sew lace to her breasts and ruching to her ribs.

There is always a pattern.

Downer Avenue Bridge

You'll find her where the river splits
and stone women hold torches to guide the way
under bridges and along brick alleyways,
where every island is a gallery for water's sculpting,

the waves pressing grass south
and placing bits of silver paper, red cans, blue glass,
symbols for something you can't decipher.
It's coincidence as much as confluence,

atoms already familiar. Remember,
together you were like water and wheel?
Gears and belts turning together to make
wood plane smooth, to turn grain into flour?

You were refracted like fish seen underwater.
Or, were you parrots, feathers brilliant under
iridescent light? You've been gone some time.
Bury your anger under the river oak.

Light a match and wander west.
You'll find her at the split, under the fire
of electric lamps. There's nothing to be afraid of.
Say a blessing. Hold out your hand.

Stars Made of Salt

for Reginald Shepherd

I look out over the crowns of trees

and see why you once said *the stars are made of salt*—

Orpheus' tears for all that's lost,

dried on a cast velvet plain,

shimmering sorrow.

Wine stains my tongue,

muddles my thoughts. You gave me meanings

for work and care, but I have mislaid them.

I was your student, Pandora,

opening her gift too early,

too clumsy to gather the lessons back in.

Bordeaux, I know, was your favorite.

You loved the spice and coursing warmth

heady in your chest

even as your cells cooled

and your heart cracked. I have filled

my glass twice tonight. It shines

like a garnet, a harp singing when I run

my finger over its rim.

Malady

The doctor takes a sextant measurement
of the woman's mind and finds its horizon
slanted and slipping eastward.

Her blood cells under magnification
read like a sheet of tidal forecasts, rounded
and wanting to list into moorings.
White cells gently knock into mollusks,
sound like bass drum and timpani tinkle.

The leeches on her back don't latch.
The hot glass' upside down suction
leaves them listless, sluggish.
She is a sea without current.

A nurse places her contusions under microscope,
spies oxidization under translucent skin.
She prods them with steel pincers
snickers at the woman's wince.

The woman knew her malady was weaving
into layers of seaweed, covering her corneas
and hazing her words with salt and barnacles
while she lost her appetite to tide.

She would swallow the stars for a cure,
and feel her blood bleached, white, waterlogged.

The Whaler's Wife Bakes Bread

The cupboard is full of flour
and self-loathing, so she lights the oven
for loaves of bread. The yeast is still

living, frothing full and bubbly in the bowl.
She substitutes anger for eggs
and measures teaspoons of disgust

to preserve the bread. She kneads
and kneads the dough smooth
and pliant, like bruised skin, lungs still

breathing. She sets it on the stove
to rise, makes a cup of bitter tea,
takes a chair to the window to watch

rain in sheets on the bottle glass, little
else beyond but brown grass and
thin chickens, roiling sea.

She slips into sleep, mouth agape,
dreams of him in the lantern-lit dark
carving whalebone into the shape

of a skull when the blade slips
and his body becomes carp, flopping.
When she wakes, the dough has not doubled,

still she forms loaves, tucks

them in buttered pans, abandons them

to bake. She tries to sing old hymns from her mother's

memories, but can't recall choruses.

The house takes on the smell of sour corners,

burnt rooftops. She dusts the mantle,

the cross made of seashells, the painting

of her mother, stern and thin-lipped,

but she remembers her soft hands.

Even if the bread turns hard and ungiving

under the knife, she will eat it. She will

think of her love, the bread she will bake for him.

The Dowager's Poem

Pencils trace roses laid beneath onion skin paper,
and I learn how to draw. It's as if I'm behind a fence
watching flowers grow, unable to touch them, a faint
smell of dust and graphite their perfume. My fingers curl
into links connecting with the delicate chain of history:
my mother's recipe for rose petal wine, my grandmother's
essential skill at painting china in the empty hours
her husband was at sea. Would she forgive me
for tracing my way back to her? I finish another outline,
one outer petal, and wonder if an operator would connect
me to her. It's almost dusk, and the pencil is dull.

When Billy Collins Falls for Me

He's had one too many cups
of coffee, black, and reads my poem
with a vibration in his hand.

He wants more. To know how
a woman can conceive of her
chest as an air-filled cavity,

her breasts balloons
that will carry her to printed pages
her words to the mouths

of professors elucidating her metaphors.
He searches his books, papers,
telephones on the land-line

to an editor he knew in the Midwest
in the '70s. Where else would women
have toes that point skyward

painted in glitter?
He finds my address, an old one,
sends letters of verbs

and parakeets. The man who receives them
wonders who the sender is, obsessed with the smell
of poltergeists, who omits his return address.

After Sitting with Christopher Smith's *Still Life*

I expect she'd speak in stock phrases
that would hover over her head
in pink balloons, wanting to please.

If she weren't carved from granite,
her hands would be clenched
and her back stick straight.

Her open eyes would be painted white,
and her hair would fall loose
across her breasts.

Probably,
her hips would be more narrow,
draped in duponi silk.

Isn't she more interesting
on her side, her belly sagging
a little toward the bed?

Her Sailor's Whimsy

Her dresser was covered
in shell boxes showing off
green limpets and cebu beauties,
white nassas and tan marginellas.
In each an ivory whimsy:
small combs for her hair in the shape
of seagulls and starfish, brooches
that looked like conches,
and combs with coral handles and teeth
as sharp as shark fins. He measured
and smoothed abalone into buttons
that she wore on her bodices.
When he was home, landlocked,
he wanted her to wear shimmering
green satin skirts, pale blue silk
blouses, let her hair fall loose
in wide curls. She was aghast
at first, but acquiesced. He braided
Venetian pearls into her strands as
she sat on a stool, reading him books
about knots and sextants. She let
him to pierce her ears to wear bobbles
of nautica lineata that dangled as they
danced on sturdy wood floors.
Always before he left again, the captain's

bell ringing brass and sharp through town,

he sewed another heart onto her pillow,

clear glass beads again purple velvet.

She woke from her naps impressed

by them, red and puffy-eyed, smelling

salt from her open windows, pulling shells

from her hair for days.

The Human Cannonball Recalls His Boyhood

His childhood was all tenements: humans stuffed like rags in a barrel with explosive scents like paprika and sweat. His world was brown tea and abandonment. Every boiling pot breathed the ghosts of his father and the mice his mother drowned in the sink. She calmed him with spoonfuls of gunpowder. It tasted like flying. He asked for more, elbowing his sister and brother from the table. All summer his sweat stank of ammunition, as he grew afraid of matches and the cook stove fire. He jumped from ever taller surfaces, the other boys were owls who craned their necks to watch. He learned to roll when he missed the landing, dreamed of feathers, capes, streamers. He taught his sister to sew sheets to catch him, his brother to safely light fuses. He saved for a second-hand cannon and a train painted red and gold. Every time he flies over the crowd, he sees his mother's face, waves at girls wearing white lace dresses. Every flight is higher, farther.

This Long Winter

what she meant when she said *hurt*

was the wind was screaming through her branches

and when he said *quiet*

he meant the silence that lives between lath and plaster

the snow falling on the pines

and the nest left bare and dangling

her lips stained with wine

his hand clenching the fork

what she meant by *feed*

what he meant by *full*

the darkness sliding over the table

candles not lit and the light burned out

her muffled breath

his pursed lips

Barnacles

When we lift the boat out of the water for the season, the barnacles are a blur on its rounded hull. We must scrape them from the wood with steel, completely unlike a cat running its rough tongue along its leg. I expect the tool to make sparks as each animal comes loose, to be drenched in wet splinters, the spit of crustaceans. I imagine my hand is a claw slashing away at small-minded politicians, bomb-marked landscapes, protesters' badly-spelled epithets. I daydream about cocoons, creatures with short, definite lives. How austere we would be gliding from one sweet flower to another, laying opaque eggs before falling to a forest floor. The boat's bottom is burnished and brown again. My muscles are brittle under my skin. I return home to soften in a tub of fresh water, its steam scented with salt and the bodies of mollusks I've erased.

Her Husband's Fishing

Kneeling, she contemplates the surface
of the pond, reflecting a broad spectacle of sky.
She wishes he hadn't died yesterday, and she looks
for his face in the clouds, the leaves at the bottom
of the muddy water. She recalls his creel
hanging in the garage, the fish he brought home,
how still they were, their scales. She sits back,
breathes the crisp air as if it were an apple
she could choke on. A tangy bite, a cough, falling
headlong into the pond. She wonders about
the dormant green lacewing eggs, the larvae
that will hatch this spring, crawl up the mud.
He always said they made the best bait.
Her apron dotted with grease
from frying the fillets he carved. The resolution
she would never eat trout again. The feeling of
the white flesh melting on her tongue and butter.

When She is Landlocked

Hinges on her ribcage
let her heart and mind
mingle before they
crumbled, fell into circles of
sown sweet pea seeds.

She latched her chest tight
as a hatch all winter as if
rouge waves were a constant
concern—fate's harsh breath
over the surface of her life.

She spends those months in auburn
virginity whispering vespers
in a curtain-dark room.
She fills her days with clocks
stopped at one, the first whole number.

In spring, sweet peas masquerade
as small blue happinesses. Her rib-
cage stands open for starlings
to peck at her lungs as she hangs sheets
she calls white. The birds she calls sin.

What Will Keep Us Alive

Even the worms that push to the surface in spring
extol the wonders of ground thaw,
sun pushing downward through the dirt.
It's generosity, the robins must think, as a buffet
spreads before them, who subsisted on dry berries.
Everything happens in accordance, as Thoreau found
in his walks around Walden, noting the temperature,
the blooming dates of bladderworts and saxifrage,
the time that buttercups and asters went to seed.
How extravagant, even the simple unfolding of a bud
this time of year. The robins note it, as they
search for twigs and grass to build a crib.
How much we want to remain, a watcher
of unleafed branches, an evader of taxes,
listening to the trill of redwing blackbirds.

To My Friend Who Pets Bees in Her Garden

after "Honeybee Swarming a Floral Hive Cluster" glass orb by
Paul Stankard

Be happy these are encased in glass—
clearly if you tried to touch them
a sweet sting would tell it true:
their honey as sacred as their buzz.
Yes, delphinium seldom grow
so close to hives, but listen,
their petal's blue protects from sun
catches rain before
it hits the comb. You wonder
about metaphor—the glass
sphere, the number of bees, nineteen,
the way they all seem to fly north, then east.
Each bee made of at least fifteen drops
of glass, each hexagon precise and paper-thin.
Stop counting, I tell you. Have faith.
You say it is just sand, but no. This
time, it's honey.

Notes

The phrase "Girl in pink on a milk white horse" in "Why the Garcias Never Attended the Circus after 1942" is from Rachel Field's poem "Equestrienne."

"The Summer Her Boyfriend Suffered Lycanthropy" and "Her Knack for Flicking Matches" were inspired by Jon Dee Graham's music on his album *Spooklight*, available on Bandcamp.com.

"The Human Cannonball Recalls His Boyhood" is based on an unaccredited photo of a human cannonball preforming at the Steel Pier in Atlantic City, NJ.

Thank You

My husband Paul, who has supported me on this crazy poeting journey even though I have yet to get rich. We are rich in love.

My family, who tolerate my lack of rhymes and sideways manner of writing about them.

My sistas, Ruth Foley, Rebecca Longster, Julie Manon, Jess Bane Robert, Mary Senior Hardwood, and Kathleen Clancy, whose creativity, resilience, love and support inspire me daily.

My workshop, reading, and writing partner, Donna Vorreyer.

Those whose groups I have drifted in and out of, but whose support has been unwavering: the Stonecoast Writing Program, Peter Murphy's Writing Getaway, The Connecticut River Poets, The Waiting 4 the Bus Poetry Collective, Binders Full of Women Poets, Submit Bitches, my Poem-a-Thon supporters, and Nina Corwin and Al DeGenova's Traveling Molly's Reading Series.

Lastly, Erin and the lovely folks at Sundress, who enjoyed my work so much they to put it into print. I am very grateful you found me.

About the Author

Kristin LaTour grew up in the Sonoran desert surrounded by mountains in Tucson, spent her early adulthood beside Lake Superior, and has settled in the prairie of Illinois near Chicago. Along the way, she learned to love all the shades of green and blue in the world, the feel of 118°F heat and -50°F cold. She has found she can always put on another sweater, but she can only strip down to what God gave her. She has published three chapbooks, most recently *Agoraphobia* with dancing girl press (2013). Her poetry has appeared in journals such as *Fifth Wednesday, Cider Press Review, MiPOesias*, and *Massachusetts Review* and the anthology *Obsession: Sestinas in the 21st Century*. Kristin teaches at Joliet Jr. College and lives with her fiction-writing husband in the beautiful city of Aurora, IL. Readers can find more at kristinlatour.com.

* 9 7 8 1 9 3 9 6 7 5 2 5 5 *